I0503407

BULLSEYE!
GETTING THE RIGHT MESSAGE TO THE RIGHT AUDIENCE

DAVE HALLS

Copyright © 2016 by Dave Halls

All rights reserved. No portion of this book may be reproduced, stored in a retrieval system, or transmitted in any form or by any means – electronic, mechanical, photocopy, recording, scanning, or other – except for brief quotations in critical reviews or articles, without the prior written permission of the author.

First Printing· 2016

ISBN: 978-1517268060

Published By Halls Global Limited
901 Hermes Commercial Centre
4 Hillwood Road, Tsim Sha Tsui
Hong Kong

DEDICATION

To my lovely wife Amy, who believed in the vision of this project
and was a support from beginning to end.

"Having been a business coach for over 20 years, I know that Dave Halls' methodology is the best way for companies and individuals to increase their success 200%. His approach is scientific, down to earth and creates real results. Start using his communication strategies today!"

Dr Todd Eller, Professor, Los Angeles College District

"What a splendid book! A brilliant five step process to build an effective message for any type of communication medium. It teaches anyone how to develop the right message for the right audience. Every person should own a copy of "Bullseye!" - it is a great resource that is packed with actionable strategies to fast impact your life, work and dreams."

Rene Kamstra, International communication expert, author, speaker and media personality

"Are you ready to take full control of your destiny? Choosing to master the art of communication is exactly where to begin. Bullseye gives you the clarity, foundation, and plan to bring your ability to express yourself to another level, in the numerous channels that are available in today's connected world. Prepare to separate yourself from the pack and stand out from the rest."

Tom Beal, speaker, author and founder of Make Today Great

"Bullseye!" by Dave Halls really does hit its mark. If you're looking to learn the skills required to really connect with your audience, then "Bullseye!" is required reading. From the framework, to the medium and language, Dave covers every aspect with great detail, and in an easy to understand fashion."

John Chow, author, blogger, speaker and entrepreneur

"*Bullseye!* takes the mystery out of what makes good communication and reveals what you can do to become a great communicator. That's why I like Dave Halls' book "Bullseye!"."

From the foreword by Dr Joe Vitale, author, speaker, hypnotic marketer, movie star and musician

DAVE HALLS

CONTENTS

Foreword 1

Introduction 3

A simple framework for communicating 10

A powerful method for communicating 15

The method in action 40

The medium and its language 47

Becoming a great communicator 54

DAVE HALLS

FOREWORD

Step back for a moment and consider all the things you do in your personal and business life.

I'll bet one of the most important elements is communication. You might need to send an email, Facebook message, conduct a meeting, or have a simple conversation. Or perhaps brief a client, prepare an information pack, generate sales materials, record a video or develop a web site. All of these are communication.

Yet for all the communication that is going on in our lives, the majority of us don't seem to do it well. We end up doing poor communication which then leads to poor outcomes.

Just the other day I heard about a friend in a board meeting. She noticed that everyone seemed lost, the flow of conversation was rambling, and nothing was determined or achieved. Do you know what let this person down?

Poor communication.

And yet you'd think that we should all be naturally good communicators. After all, we've been communicating since we were born.

But sadly we're not. Perhaps that's because good communication takes time and effort. Or the skill is hard to quantify and there are not a lot people teaching this stuff to the average person. The ability to be a great communicator is then left to intuition or those who seem to be more "gifted" than others.

That's why I like Dave Halls' book "Bullseye!".

"Bullseye!" takes the mystery out of what makes good communication and reveals what you can do to become a great communicator.

Dave has been in the communication game for many years and understands the elements that make up a good piece of communication. He also knows how to use those elements to craft a tight message and aim it with precision at the target audience using the right media. Further, he is passionate about sharing his knowledge with others.

In "Bullseye!" you'll learn:

- The important elements that go on during a communication where you have an audience interacting with your message

- A simple 5 step method that uses these elements to craft a tight, relevant message that is targeted to your audience

- About the different ways media work and how they influence the way you need to communicate when using them

- Practical examples of how this method applies across different media like writing, videos, social media and so on

The value in this book is in how it takes a complex topic and explains this simply so that you can start making practical steps towards becoming a great communicator. You'll develop a fundamental understanding of how communication works that you can apply in any context.

The best thing you can do is to read, learn and apply.

Read this book and get faster and better results.

It all begins with a turn of the page…

- Dr Joe Vitale

INTRODUCTION

When did you last send a message that didn't get through to your audience?

Perhaps it was a sales letter that failed to resonate with your prospect. Or a document that confused your reader in its description of a complex technical concept. Or even a simple youtube clip that started but never finished...

Have you ever delivered a message that came out the wrong way?

Maybe you included some inaccurate data in a quick verbal update to a colleague you were passing in the corridor at work? Or sent a confused message in a hastily written email? How about wandering all over a topic in front of a group of disinterested accountants following a lunch break?

We've all been there.

Despite the best of intentions, and without the right preparation, we can send out the wrong message or hit the wrong audience. Right down to a simple skype message, phone call, or coffee catch-up with a few poorly chosen words.

As long as we are interacting with people, our words, images and actions are going to influence how others perceive us. Others will make decisions based on how they perceive or understand us from the way we communicate.

Regardless of whether we have the message or audience right.

Yet most of the time we often "fluke" or "wing" our interactions without much thought, happy to live with the consequences. Consequences that could be stalling our achievements and severely limiting our success.

An important part of achieving success is knowing how to communicate well.

In fact, to become truly successful in what you choose, it is important to step up and become a GREAT communicator. Someone who knows how to carefully craft a message and then deliver it powerfully through whatever medium is at hand.

Great communicators achieve incredible success for themselves and others.

Just think of people who have served in industry like Steve Jobs, Bill Gates and Jack Welch. Or leaders in the motivational industry like Jim Rohn, Brian Tracey, Tony Robbins or Chet Holmes. Consider politicians like Ronald Regan, Bob Hawke, Bill Clinton, Barack Obama, or David Cameron. Or religious leaders like Billy Graham, Rick Warren, and Joel Osteen.

These leaders in their field would not have succeeded without having great communication skills that they developed over time.

But being a great communicator is not limited to people who want to be the next Ronald Reagan or Tony Robbins. It's freely available to anyone who is willing to put in the work at becoming a great communicator. Anyone who wants to make a difference in any facet of life.

How often have you heard about:

- Someone suffering from a medical condition that could have been prevented if they were able to describe their condition better, or if their doctor was able to explain the issue in plain language?

- A government response to a disaster that could have saved many more lives if there was better communication between agencies and people on the ground?

- Highly emotional problems in the work place that have grown out of a misunderstanding from poor communication?

- A broken personal relationship that would have been avoided if there was better communication?

- A missed business opportunity simply because an idea or concept was not explained well?

These are everyday situations that need someone like you to make a difference through great communication skills. These skills can achieve so many things that are essential to everyday life.

So what are great communication skills?

A set of skills that you perfect over time that enable you to connect with an audience and share a message accurately to achieve your communication purpose.

One key skillset is what I call being able to hit the bullseye. Hit the RIGHT audience with the RIGHT message.

My goal in this short book is to show what you need to do to hit the bullseye in your communication activities by:

- Explaining the key elements that go on in any kind of communication

- Describing a process that uses these elements powerfully to get great communication results

- Showing you how to apply this process across all types of communication

You'll get a simple, but powerful, system that will help you focus your message and target your audience with confidence every time you apply it.

But before we get into this, let's set some foundations to help you understand how this works.

CHOOSING THE RIGHT PATH

Often when people think about becoming a communicator they are focusing on one kind of delivery. This could be giving a speech, writing an email, delivering a webinar, writing a sales letter or presenting in a video.

There tends to be a focus on the medium first when talking about communication.

You can see this by taking a quick survey of your online bookstore in the communication section. There are plenty of books on "How to deliver great presentations", "Secrets of Copywriting", "Putting together your first technical manual", "YouTube marketing" or "podcasting 101".

Therefore, each book takes you on a unique path to being great in a particular medium. For four books covering four different media you'll get four unique paths, none of which are consistent with each other.

To become good at communicating across different media you'll need to learn a lot of different methods.

What if there was a simpler way to become good - no GREAT! - at communicating across all media that uses one simple approach? One path that can help you become a great communicator regardless of media?

That's where this system comes in.

Instead of starting with the medium (or delivery method), it starts with a focus on developing a message. Then the system helps you choose the best available medium to deliver that message. It gets you to consider key elements that will help you make the right decisions about how to deliver your message in the best possible way.

With this system, you'll be able to create success when preparing any kind of communication piece. This could be when sending a message through a blog, video, sales letter, technical manual, podcast, webinar or social media posting.

And you'll have a solid path to becoming a great communicator.

At this point you might wonder what I mean by a "great communicator".

BECOMING A GREAT COMMUNICATOR

A great communicator is someone who can craft a clear message and then adapt that message to suit the best medium for the target audience. A great communicator understands the language of the medium and how to mold the message to work brilliantly through that medium without losing the essence of the message.

Having said this, the term "great communicator" might be a little misleading.

That's because it could imply an end point that you can reach. A point where you have "made it" and so don't need to develop any more. This is misleading.

Great communicators are often very humble because they are not always great. They have their off days where their message gets lost. And there are times when they review what they have delivered and want to give up.

Paradoxically this is what makes them great.

Great communicators have a humility that allows them to see new ways of improving their communication skills. They will always review their work and actively find areas to improve their skills.

That's why understanding the principles and the language of communication is so important. These offer guidelines that can guide a communicator to continually evaluate and innovate so that they are continually fresh in their approach.

This mindset of being open to constant improvement is essential to becoming a great communicator. Supported by this mindset, I'd like to see you become someone who:

- Understands and can control the key elements in any communication

- Has a process that allows you to efficiently create great communication pieces

- Can comfortably deliver your message across different media to suit your audience

7

GETTING THE MOST FROM THIS BOOK

This book has four major sections to help you become a great communicator:

- Key elements of communication
- Communication process
- Applying the communication process
- Understanding the language of the medium

The first chapter introduces you to a framework that you need to understand around communication. It includes the key elements to be aware of in any communication. Make sure you understand these elements because we'll use these to show you steps to take in your successful communication.

The second chapter explains the step-by-step process that I use when preparing a communication piece. It takes the elements I described in the first section and puts them into a process that will set you up with a great message and ensure a successful delivery.

You'll get the process that I use when writing blogs, scripting videos, drafting sales emails, posting on social media and more. It's a practical step-by-step guide that will set you up with a great message and ensure a successful delivery.

The third chapter shows how you can apply the communication process to a few different communication pieces: a blog, video, and Facebook post. It captures the thinking that's involved whilst following the process described in the previous section.

The fourth chapter introduces you to the language of different media. As you read through this book, you'll find out that each medium has its own language and different way of delivering a message. Being able to use this language whilst delivering your message will turbo charge your effectiveness. This chapter aims to introduce you to the key points for future study.

My advice is to read this book from the beginning through to the end. You'll build yourself a valuable picture of how good communication works and learn how to develop the skills to become a great communicator.

Later you can come back to specific sections for reference.

Let's start by looking at a simple framework for communicating.

1
A SIMPLE FRAMEWORK FOR COMMUNICATING

Whenever you communicate with someone - whether in person, through the Web, on video or in print - you will find a number of important elements in play:

- Purpose, which is what drives your communication
- Audience, which is the person or people you are communicating with
- Media, which is the means to deliver your message
- Content, which is the subject matter that makes up your message

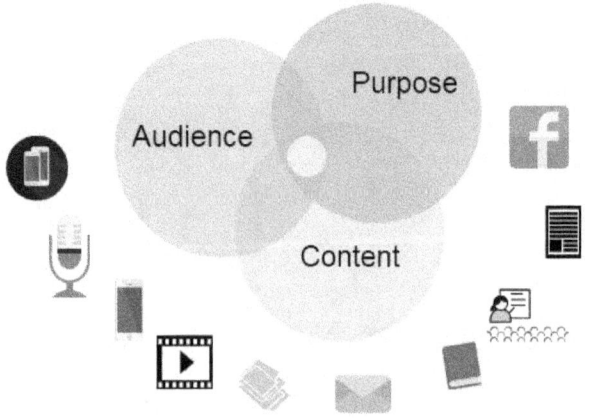

These elements form a simple framework from which you can understand how communication works to be effective or not effective.

PURPOSE

Every interaction is driven by a purpose.

Sometimes this purpose is obvious whilst at other times it is not.

Let's say you have a casual conversation with a stranger at a crossing whilst waiting for the Walk sign to go green. Behind that interaction can lie any number of purposes. It might be to fill time, be courteous to another person, enjoy talking or share your frustration at the time it takes for the light to turn green.

Whether you like it or not, there will be a purpose that sits behind your communication.

We tend not to worry too much about the purpose that drives casual communication to the point that we don't even think about it.

But we do need to think carefully about our purpose when it comes to crafting an important piece of communication. It is, after all, the reason for communicating in the first place. Without a purpose, there's probably no need to communicate.

If you want to be effective when communicating, you must consciously know your purpose throughout the interaction. Your purpose allows you to plan your communication piece well, deliver it well, and evaluate its effectiveness after delivering it.

A purpose states what you wish your piece of communication to achieve for your audience.

It is also important to write a purpose down. There are lots of good reasons for this:

- It is easier to see inconsistencies if they exist in the purpose when written down on paper

- Others can see the purpose and be "on the same page"

- A purpose in your head can easily change over time whilst a purpose on paper will not change

As a communicator, a purpose will save you time, keep you on track and help in making good decisions around the kind of material to include in the communication.

AUDIENCE

There is no communication or interaction without an audience.

Even if you have someone in the same room but not listening or taking in what you have to say, there is no communication.

That's why audience is a critical element to be aware of when talking about how communication works.

Knowing your audience helps you craft a message that can resonate with them when they listen, watch or read your communication piece. This makes it more challenging to communicate because all audiences are different.

Later in this book we'll cover how you can get to understand your audience so you can target your message more effectively to them.

MEDIA

There are lots of ways to get your message across. These can include a blog, video, podcast, book, report, email and more. They are collectively known as "media" or individually as a "medium".

Each medium has its own language and is good for communicating some things and poor for communicating other things. Video is great for communicating less detailed information in pictures that can be consumed quickly. But it is poor for delivering detailed information such as tables and detailed graphs.

This is because we tend to consume different media differently.

Media is an important element of communication because it is a means of getting your message across. By knowing the best medium for the type of message you want to communicate and understanding the language of that medium, you can dramatically improve your chance of communication success.

CONTENT

Content refers to the raw information you have available to use when crafting your message. It is something you collect based on how relevant it is to your purpose and audience.

You can use the content to learn about the subject and think through how best to reshape it into a message that fits your purpose.

Some people often think content is just something you collect, copy and paste into a communication piece.

What they don't realize is that that content was originally written for a different purpose and audience to your current purpose and audience. Copying and pasting that content into your new piece will be like pushing a square through a round hole.

Your role as a communicator is to later take this content and make it relevant to your current purpose and audience.

CONCLUSION

Now that we've spent time studying the key elements that happen during a communication, you might be wondering how this is useful for becoming a great communicator.

These key elements make up a framework for understanding how successful - and unsuccessful - communication works. It allows you to see what is going on in a communication that is causing it to be successful or unsuccessful. Watch these elements closely during an interaction and you will see that their nature is unique to the situation you are in.

If you're in a communication situation and you see it through the lens of the key elements... purpose, audience, media and content... then perhaps you can control that communication more effectively?

For example, let's imagine that you are expected to deliver a message to a room full of bankers. You'll prepare your communication piece using a language that resonates with bankers. However, at the last minute you find out that you have to deliver that same message to a room full of mechanics.

An ordinary communicator would not make any change in how they communicate.

A great communicator will see that one of the key elements (audience) has just changed, requiring an adjustment in the language so that it resonates with mechanics instead of bankers.

Taking this further, let's imagine that your purpose in a new communication piece is to convince an iPhone user to use a new feature. To meet that purpose you might adopt a persuasive approach. But what happens if the purpose changes to just explain the new feature? You are better off switching from persuasive to explanatory mode when delivering the information.

See how the framework operates?

The key elements are always present, but they can change. As they change, you need to make adjustments to keep your communication on course, just like a GPS system makes adjustments in its directions when the co-ordinates change.

A great communicator will see these elements in play during a communication and manipulate these to their advantage.

For example, if you are clear on your message but your audience changes, you should be able to quickly modify how you present that message to them. If you prepare a message for video but find out your audience can only access audio, then a great communicator can use that information to adjust the message for a different medium.

We'll see how this works in the next section when we look at a process for communicating powerfully by using these key elements.

2

A POWERFUL METHOD FOR COMMUNICATING

You can waste a lot of time trying to develop a communication piece.

Firstly, you may not know where to start. Should you just sit in front of a computer screen and start typing? Or hit record on your camera and start talking whatever comes out to the video camera? What about writer's block?

Secondly, you may not be sure what you want to communicate or how. Which is a worry - if you're not sure of what you wish to communicate, how can you expect your audience to understand the message you put out? That will lead to lots of time-costly revisions.

Thirdly, you might wonder what elements to focus on. Structure? Spelling? Pronunciation? If you get this in the wrong order then you can also waste a lot of time.

Finally, how can you know when you've got enough information or content to use?

Developing a short, concise communication piece doesn't have to be that difficult.

That's why I use a five step process whenever I need to create a communication piece. I apply it to writing blogs, developing web pages, organizing videos, writing emails and any other communication opportunity I get.

This is a scalable process. You can spend a few moments working your way through it for a small communication opportunity. Or you can spend a few hours or days for a much bigger communication piece.

Regardless, the benefit comes from working through the process so you can think clearly about what you are communicating in the right order. This will save you time and give you great clarity.

The five steps are:
1. Gather your "intel"
2. Structure your message
3. Flesh out your message
4. Review your work
5. Deliver

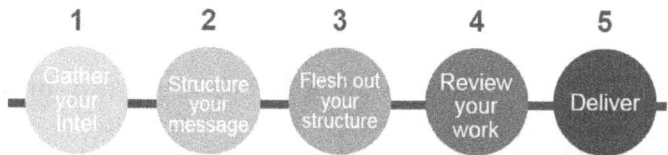

Throughout this chapter we'll look at this process in detail.

GATHERING YOUR INTEL

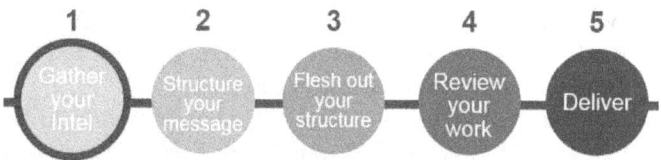

In all the great spy novels and movies, the main characters will spend a lot of their time getting "intelligence" on the people they need to catch. The right intelligence - "intel" for short - is critical for their success. With the wrong - or even some - missing intel a spy can fail miserably.

You can fail miserably in your communication if you start before gathering the right intel. The consequences may not be as high as they are in the espionage game, but a failure in communicating properly can lead to a lost opportunity, stalled career progression, relationship breakdown, rejection and more.

That's why I've set "gathering your intel" as the first step in the communication process. It's critical to gather the right intel before you start putting together a piece of communication. Good intel gives you greater confidence in the decisions you are making to shape and deliver your communication.

I'd like to share with you four types of intel that you must gather to prepare for a successful communication piece:

- Purpose - you need to clarify this

- Audience - you need to understand this

- Media - you need to choose the best medium for your message

- Content - you need to gather appropriate content that you can use when writing your message later

Clarify your purpose

Your purpose is like a mission statement. It outlines what you need to achieve by using the communication you are about to create.

Remember how earlier I talked about communication being purpose driven? It's important when drafting your communication piece to be clear about your purpose.

Your purpose needs to be easy to measure. When drafting a purpose I like to include three elements:

- Action word

- Audience

- What you want to achieve.

This removes any doubt about what I am aiming to achieve through this communication.

Let's take a look at one example:

"Convince home based business operators why they need to become great communicators."

You'll see that I have included the action word "convince", the audience "home based business operators", and what I want to achieve, which is for them to "see the need to become great communicators"

There are some good reasons why you will want to have these three elements in your purpose statement.

Firstly, having the action word will later help you when choosing how to structure your message. The word "convince" flags to the communicator that one needs to persuade, which gets one thinking about persuasive structures that might be useful.

Secondly, including the audience focuses the communicator on the audience and gets them thinking about how to understand that audience. You need to understand your audience because this will impact the language you choose and what media you opt for.

A final point to make about having a purpose is that you must write it down. There are lots of good reasons for this:

- It is easier to see inconsistencies if they exist in the purpose when written down on paper

- Others can see the purpose and be on the same page

- A purpose in the head can easily change over time whilst a purpose on paper will stay the same

- A purpose will save the communicator time, keep them on track and help them to make good decisions around the kind of material to include in the communication

---

INTEL ACTION STEP 1: Write down your purpose on a piece of paper or on screen where you can see it whilst preparing your communication piece.

Understand your audience

With your purpose written down, you should know who your audience is. But that's not enough.

The more you understand your audience, the better positioned you will be to tailor your message so that it resonates with them and contains relevant information. There are so many ways to understand an audience. A lot has been written about this over the years. My main point here is that you make every effort to understand your audience regardless of how you choose to go about this.

A simple, starting point that I use when thinking about my audience is to find out what are my audience's:

- Needs

- Attitudes

- Wants

Give your audience what they need and you'll find that they are most likely to tune in to your message. There are lots of tricks around making content "compelling", but I think this is the most effective approach possible.

When giving your audience what they need it's important to give it in a way that doesn't turn them away. That's why knowing their attitude is so important. If you are about to deliver news on a subject that your audience is negative about, you'll know to look for a way that neutralizes that negativity. If you know someone is afraid of a new idea you want to introduce, you can take that into account and deliver the news more gently.

Finally, if you can give your audience just that little bit extra – what they might want but actually don't need – then you'll keep them happy.

I always start thinking about my audience in terms of their needs, attitudes and wants.

But this is just the start point in beginning to understand your audience. There are other things to consider such as their demographic, education/experience level, industry, socio economic group, gender and more.

There are also methods for understanding your audience in a lot of detail such as developing a persona or avatar of who you are communicating with. Or a customer insight diagram if in marketing.

Regardless of how, the aim is to develop a clear picture of who you are communicating to. That will allow you to communicate with a lot more focus.

INTEL ACTION STEP 2: Identify your audience and get key information about who you are communicating with. Start with the "needs, attitudes and wants" and progress to further details. Perhaps develop a persona to help visualize your audience.

Choose the best medium for your message

There are lots of ways to get a message across:

- Paper document
- Web
- Email
- Video
- Social media
- Poster
- And more...

Each of these is a medium with its own unique language.

For example, the language of Twitter is a one or two sentence statement or question whilst the language of video is moving pictures. The language of podcasting is sound whilst the language of posters is images and text.

Each medium is best for communicating a certain type of information. For example paper documents are great for communicating information in static graphs whilst video isn't.

When thinking of the available media for your communication piece you need to consider:

- What is the best medium to get your message across?

- What is the language of that medium?

The best medium to use depends on two things that you need to juggle. The first is your audience's preference for getting information. If they tune in better to video than they do email you should choose video. The second thing is what medium you think is going to communicate the information best. If you have a table or graph to demonstrate you won't want to use video because it won't work as effectively as a paper document or pdf.

A lot of people think they can pull together a video and post it on youtube and it will be an instant hit. But if they use language that does not work for the medium (such as twitter language), the audience will just tune out and miss your message.

A lot of people can write and send an email and assume that because it was sent that the information was read. But many don't realize that a reeeeaaallly long email they have just sent can turn some people off. Maybe even their entire audience.

Here is a quick rundown of popular media and what kind of information they are best at communicating and what kind of language they use.

Medium	Best at	Language
Email	Written messages of medium length	Conversational, active writing style, plain language – simple words, short sentences. Not too much information.
Video	Action stories and messages with little detail	Moving images, limited still images.

Medium	Best at	Language
Podcasting	Stories	Sounds in terms of words (the onomatopoeic effect), sound effects, mood music or atmosphere sounds etc.
Twitter	Short, sharp informative messages (no more than two sentences)	One or two sentences – no more. Needs to be succinct and in an active style.
Web pages	Providing information people are seeking, such as answers to questions.	Plain language, i.e., plain rather than fancy words, short sentences rather than long sentences. Active rather than passive sentences and so on.

INTEL ACTION STEP 3: Decide on the best media available to use for your communication piece according to your audience's preference and the kind of message you are delivering.

Gather the right content for your communication piece

There is still more "intel" that you need to gather before you're in a good position to start crafting your communication piece. That extra intel comes in the form of raw content.

Raw content is that collection of research material that you will draw on to create your own content to fit your unique purpose and satisfy your unique audience. You will use raw content to learn about your subject and gather raw data that you can use when crafting your unique message.

Raw data can include references to the Internet, videos, pictures or documents.

Some very amateur communicators think that once they have collected this content, it is ready for them to use. They think they can do the equivalent of a copy and paste into their communication piece. They fail to realize that, apart from probably infringing copyright, this raw content was written to satisfy a different purpose and audience to their own project. Blindly copying this into their new piece will not meet their purpose and it won't satisfy their audience. This will fail.

The raw content is the reference material that you can take and later rework so that it fits your own purpose and satisfies the needs, attitudes and wants of your targeted audience. This is something we'll look at later.

There is a lot of content out in the world – just think of what is available on the Internet. So how can you decide what is relevant to use when preparing a communication?

Know your purpose and audience.

Your purpose will influence what kind of content you may need to include in your communication. It will give you a starting point from which to choose content. Then as you gather or consider further content, you can qualify it against whether that is relevant to what you need to communicate to meet your purpose.

Added to this, your understanding of the audience is going to help you choose the level of detail in the content you might want to gather. For example, if you know your audience knows a lot about a particular subject, you may not need to include much detail about that content. If they don't know much detail, you may need to gather a lot more detail.

Good communicators know that just gathering the right content is not enough to create a great communication. This step is about gathering the raw data of information they have from which to work on.

Once they have the right content they need to "shape" it into a flow of information that is logical and meaningful to the audience.

We'll look at that in the next section.

> **INTEL ACTION STEP 4**: Draw together raw content that you can use to structure and craft your message, based on your purpose and audience. Identify what you know, don't know, and need to learn to communicate your message well

Conclusion

This completes gathering your intel.

The point of gathering intel first before shaping and structuring your communication is to cover all the bases that are important to creating a good piece of communication. That's why we covered:

- Purpose - which provides a yardstick to measure your effectiveness before, during and after the communication

- Audience - which focuses you on who you are communicating with so that you can resonate with them and give them information that is most helpful

- Media - so you can choose the best method of delivering your message based on your audience and the type of material you are communicating

- Content - so you can do the right research to be comfortable communicating your message

Armed with this information, you are ready to start creating your message or content.

In the following chapters I'll show you how to:

- Shape your message with the right structure

- Flesh out your structure

- Review your work

- Deliver your communication piece with confidence

Stay tuned!

Structuring Your Message

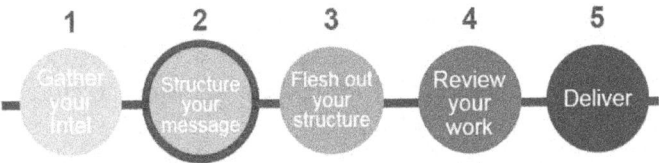

At this stage you should be clear about your purpose, understand your audience, have chosen the medium to use and have enough raw content from which to know about your subject. You have gathered the intel that will help you craft a great piece of communication. So you are now ready to start working on it.

The best way to start is by developing a structure.

What is structure?

Structure refers to the logical flow of ideas that you have in your piece from sentence to sentence, paragraph to paragraph or picture to picture. It's a flow that occurs at the section and heading level right down to the sentence level.

Just to confuse you... there's also a thing called a superstructure, which refers to a high level structure that only outlines the generic flow. It captures the flow at the heading levels but isn't concerned about the flow of ideas between paragraphs and sentences.

One example of a superstructure is the standard sales letter template that provides you with a series of headings or directions of what to write in a particular order that is deemed persuasive.

If you were using this superstructure, creating a sales letter would involve fleshing out this superstructure with content that follows the flow set by the superstructure. It would then be up to you to flesh out this structure further with your own logical flow using content that is appropriate to your purpose and audience.

The sales letter is only one example of a superstructure. In the document world superstructures are often referred to as "templates". These can include a business case, proposal, user guide or software architecture templates. When writing stories there are superstructures based around telling a powerful story based on the three act Hollywood narrative. When writing news stories there are superstructures like the "inverted" pyramid.

So how do you choose a structure or superstructure?

Choosing a structure or superstructure

It all comes down to the purpose.

If your purpose is to get people to buy a new product, then a sales letter superstructure will probably be a great starting point. If you need to "explain how to print a document", an instruction guide superstructure might be great. If you want to introduce you and your ideas at a conference talk, a story superstructure might be a good way to go.

Great communicators know how to draw on existing superstructures and then tailor these to their own purpose so that their message is more impressive.

Another thing to note about structures is that they can be unique to a specific medium.

Let's think back to the earlier sales letter superstructure example. That will work for a printed document or perhaps an email. But you would not use it if creating a video sales letter. Since video works differently and there are other "proven" ways of presenting information, you will need to draw on a video sales letter template / superstructure. This would need to adopt language and style of the video medium.

Developing your own structure

To develop your structure, you'll need a few things:

- Your purpose (which should have been written down from earlier steps)

- An understanding of your audience (at least their needs, attitudes and wants)

- Clear choice of your medium

- Content

Sound familiar?

There's a good reason why we spent so much time earlier looking at gathering intel. That information will guide you into creating a clear, concise structure.

Begin by revising your purpose and refreshing your understanding of the audience.

As you revisit your purpose, look at the action word. This is a great flag to suggest what kind of superstructure or template you might like to start with. If your purpose is to "convince your prospect to buy a new product", then "convince" would suggest the need for a persuasive approach and a sales letter template might be a pretty good starting point. If it is to explain how to print a document, "explain" might suggest an instructional type of document like a work instruction.

Now consider what medium you have chosen to use.

If you are using video, that's when you might choose a video sales letter template to start with.

Now comes the fun bit.

Superstructures are are fallible. Just because they might be a "superstructure", they are not always super. As you start with your superstructure, you can start evaluating whether or not it is relevant to your audience or will meet the purpose. If it doesn't, then you can modify.

You may also like to skip the superstructure step and start with a structure from scratch.

When developing a structure, I like to use a tree diagram. The best way to picture a structure is look at the table of contents for a document down to three levels of headings. Then describe under each heading what you wish to cover in that section. Then you'll have a structure.

But a word of advice and encouragement. Don't expect to get it right the first time you devise your structure. A good structure is something that happens after many attempts to get it right. Each time you might adjust the structure, you may find something new that you don't like. That's when you adjust it.

Remember to refer back to your purpose and audience whenever you make a decision around structure. Ask yourself "will this help me achieve my purpose?" and "does this serve the audience?"

Once you are satisfied with your structure after many iterations, it is ready to start fleshing it out.

FLESHING OUT YOUR STRUCTURE

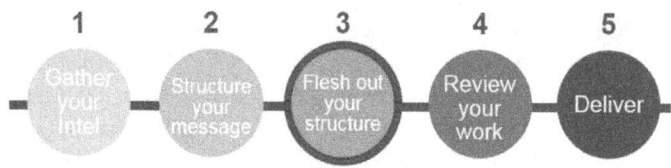

Now that you have finalized a structure you are ready to start fleshing it out.

- For writing based communications this means starting on your text

- For video communications this may involve scripting your sequence and/or the associated words you'll deliver or simply delivering it straight to camera (based on your structure or outline)

- For audio communications this may involve writing your audio script or recording (based on your structure or outline)

Fleshing out your structure is largely a matter of just writing, re-writing and re-writing until you are happy with your work. You need to produce something that aligns with your structure and fits your purpose. The ideas need to flow nicely from one point to the next. You also need to use the right language that fits your audience.

As to how you should go about doing all this…. it's really up to you.

However... before you do start hitting the keyboard or putting pen to paper, it is important to take time in understanding:

- Language of your audience
- Language of your medium
- Tools and devices available that can support you maximize your message within the medium

Communicate in the language of your audience

There are lots of reasons to do your best in understanding the audience you are pitching your communication to. One of these is so you have a good idea of the language that they use to communicate.

Business people naturally use a different language to car mechanics. People in one state can often use subtly different words or phrases to people who live in other states or territories.

Get to know what language cuts through to your audience so you can use it in your communication. If you're not sure, aim to be more general and adopt a plain language approach. Avoid words that will confuse your audience or alienate them.

Once you adopt this approach you'll find yourself resonating with your audience. You'll have a good rapport with them and then be able to communicate pretty much anything with them.

Use the language of your medium to communicate

Each medium has its own language.

Video uses moving images. Podcasts use sounds. Written material uses words on paper or the screen.

Be clear on the medium you are writing for and then use its language properly. Your message will cut through much more effectively if you do. If you don't, well... then you can diminish your ability to cut through.

Let me share an example. We know that people tune into video because of the movement it provides through moving pictures. Take away visual movement for more than a few seconds on a video and you'll lose your audience.

Recently I was shown a series of training videos produced by a leader in a particular profession. It consisted of a series of PowerPoint slides with a person talking over them. The information was great. The subject matter was really important. But no one was getting it because it was a static image that lost me and others within about four seconds.

Even if you are stuck with boring material to put on video, there are ways of giving it more movement just to make it more interesting. Switching between long shots and close up shots for a talent is one of these. Understanding this as part of the language of video is important to help you communicate better on video.

Don't waste your hard work and valuable content by not using the language of the medium.

Use the tools and devices within the medium to support getting your message out

Each medium has its own unique set of tools and devices that make it more effective in communicating the message.

Let's take a sales letter as an example.

There are writing techniques that a copy writer will use to increase the effectiveness of the sales letter. This could include specific words or phrases that are known to work – just consider the phrase "the secret they don't want you to know" as a heading. Emotive words placed at just the right spot are also a powerful device. Just as other style elements like using large bullet points, initial caps for each word in a headline, or even colors.

Let's take this further. A classic device in writing a sales letter is to use a very conversational style with all sorts of stops and starts.

For example:

"I can't wait to share this with you...

Here's a new software tool that will make you thousands in 24 hours! ...but you better hurry up. This won't be available for long.

Click below..."

Switching across to the video medium, the type of transition between scenes (a fade, dissolve, whoosh) is a device or tool you can use to keep the movement going and tell your story and impact your message.

Crossing to the podcasting medium, theme music and sound effects used at the right moment are powerful tools or devices that can help sharpen your message.

The point in all this? Get to know the tools and devices of the medium you are using to create maximum impact in the way you communicate!

Conclusion on fleshing out your structure

There are lots of ways to flesh out your structure. Don't expect to get it right first time round. As you re-read each revision, you are likely to find better ways of communicating ideas.

And you might even need to revisit the structure, which is fine.

Developing your communication is an iterative process that can take plenty of revisions before you are satisfied - particularly when you start out in this process.

Remember to use the language of your audience.

Also learn as much about the language of your medium as possible. Know how to write for paper, screen, video or audio. Start with one medium and get good at that and then progress to the next one.

Once you have finished fleshing out your communication piece, you will have something ready to review.

REVIEWING YOUR WORK

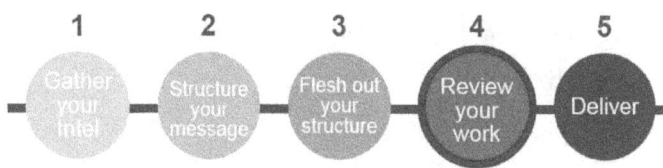

While deep in the process of creating a communication piece you'll naturally become very clear on what you wish to relay to your audience. So clear, in fact, that you will start to see what you want to see rather than what might actually be there in the message.

This is because your mind already knows what should be on the page or in the video you produce. When the actual version misses something important or includes a mistake, your mind will subconsciously correct the mistake.

This means that you won't see the problem.

But your audience will.

Your audience won't have gone through the same process that led you to the ideas that you wish to communicate. Their mind is not prepared to make the automatic correction as they consume the communication.

This is why reviewing is important.

We naturally make mistakes that we won't want to appear in our communication. Therefore, we need a process to identify those mistakes before our final version goes out. We also need a process that overcomes our mind's ability to compensate for mistakes.

There is probably not a single, correct way of reviewing. Everyone is unique in the ways they might approach the reviewing process. Different approaches suit different personalities.

However, there are some principles that I believe will help you become efficient at the review process.

I'll do this by covering:

- Reviewing mindset

- Different ways to review

- Random tips and tricks that can help you in the review process

The reviewing mindset

When given the task of reviewing someone's work, it's important to develop a particular mindset.

Thinking back to the days when I worked in a software house, it was interesting to watch the Quality Assurance (QA) guys as they performed "QA" on the software before it was finalized for release.

Their task was to find bugs in the software so that the software engineers could fix them before the company released it into the market. The QA phase became a contest between QA team members to see how many bugs they could find. They began their testing by assuming that the software was flawed but without the proof to see this. So they made it their goal to find the proof!

This was an aggressive approach. But it worked really well.

The same approach can work really well when reviewing a communication piece. Start out by assuming there is a problem with your communication piece and looking for the evidence.

Compare the actual purpose against what you need. Look at the structure of the messaging or ideas and look for inconsistencies. Or drill down to the style elements and check what is written or said against what you expect to see for word choice, sentences, paragraphs, images or statements.

With a mindset that expects problems you can more easily find them if they exist.

Different types of reviews

There are lots of ways to review a communication piece. Let me share with you what works well for me.

I believe a good starting point is to ask:

- Does the communication meet the original purpose?

- Is the communication targeted towards the audience?

If you cannot answer yes to these two questions, then you can expect to have some problems with your communication piece.

If it doesn't meet your purpose then you are wasting an opportunity by not sending the right message. If the message is not targeted effectively to the right audience, then you could be wasting your time.

There is no point looking at other elements before you can address the issue of purpose and audience.

Assuming you have your audience and purpose right, I like to focus on the structure of my communication piece next. Have I got the concepts or ideas in the right order so that it makes sense? Does this serve to make the communication piece persuasive, informative, instructive as defined in my purpose?

If there are issues with the structure, I would like to clear these up before reviewing further. I might need to remove a section or add a new section. Who knows? But I'll waste time progressing further in the review if I don't make sure that the structure is right.

Next I will turn to my style. Have I chosen the right words for my content and audience? Are the sentences I've written or spoken short and succinct? Have I avoided confusion by keeping to one idea in a paragraph? Or focused on one idea at a time in my presentation?

If I'm happy with my style I'll look at "mechanical" things like spelling, punctuation or conventions. If I am doing a speech, have I got all the pronunciations right?

Finally - if we are talking about a printed communication piece, I'll take time to focus on the formatting to see that it is consistent and helps the reader navigate through the structure of my content.

If it is a video, have I been consistent with intros, titles, musical themes, dissolves and so on. Or for a podcast, have I used the right opening and closing theme, and edited the product in the right style.

I like to run through my communication piece several times to focus on each level. This helps me actively search for problems and be thorough in my approach.

As you have seen, my review tends to focus on the communication element of my piece. Whilst this is important, there is also the technical side.

For example, when producing a video you may need to make sure your output is in a particular format, in a specified file size or uploaded to a site like youtube. And you need to make sure the rendered file works and the output is what you expected it to be.

If you're creating a printed brochure, you may need to supply it in a particular format with settings specified by your printer. There's nothing worse than getting poorly printed images because you sent a file with the wrong resolution settings.

If creating a landing page on your web site, you might need to ensure that your auto responder forms are connected to your email auto responder.

There a lots of technical things you need to review before delivering.

So how can you remember all this?

Developing your own check list

It's important to develop your own review check list of things to look for when reviewing a communication piece.

You should include on your list standard things like purpose, audience, spelling, structure, mechanics, technical and so on. But you also need to go a little deeper.

What are common everyday errors you or the creator of the communication piece you are reviewing make?

Sometimes there are common words that are misspelled, fancy words that should be avoided, or formatting errors in documents that are forgotten. Perhaps in a speech there is a particular phrase that finds its way in but that doesn't work well.

Armed with a check list, you can actively look for common mistakes to make sure they don't get through to the final output.

Don't be satisfied with only one check list.

Create one for each type of communication you create. Create a:

- Blog check list

- Speech check list

- Landing page check list

- Video check list

- Learning webinar check list

- Sales webinar check list

- Poster check list

- And so on

Why not create a check list for different occasions you find yourself in?

I've got a check list at home called "Top Ten Things To Look For In A Document One Hour Before Printing". It lists all the "important" things I can't afford to get wrong in a printed document. This is a great review aid when under pressure to put something out fast.

I've also got a check list for uploading vimeo content to make sure that descriptions are consistent across all my video listings.

The simple fact is that check lists are great for helping your review. Get ready for your communication piece with a check list that helps you deliver quality content.

Random tips and tricks

Having the right mindset, approach and check list will put you on a successful path for reviewing.

Here are a few more tips around reviewing your communication piece in no particular order.

- For written communication, check your spelling by reading your text backwards

- If you have to review your own work, give yourself time distance between finishing it and reviewing it.

- If you can't get time distance between finishing and reviewing your own work, go for geographical distance instead - leave you work desk and sit in another environment such as a work kitchen or garden

- For technical pieces such as web pages video or podcasts, test the audience experience

- It's better if you can have someone else to review your work because you'll get fresher feedback

- When asking someone for feedback, be clear about what feedback will actually be helpful - tell your reviewer something like "let me know about the structure, but don't worry about spelling as that won't be helpful at this stage"

These are just some ideas to get you thinking about how to review effectively.

At the end of the day make sure you review your work as much as it is physically possible. Remember to:

- Approach reviewing with the right mindset

- Follow a methodical approach such as the one covered earlier

- Develop check lists
- Look for ways to improve your approach to reviewing your work or somebody else's work

DELIVERING AND CREATING SUCCESS

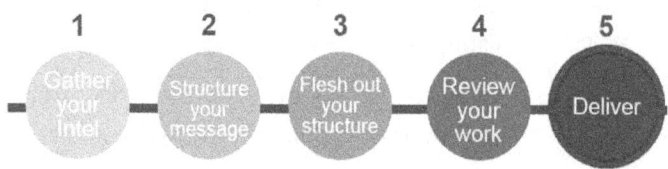

At this stage you should have reviewed your communication piece and be satisfied that it is ready to go out.

Now it is time to deliver it.

This will depend on what medium you are working in.

- If video, this might mean uploading a clip to vimeo or youtube and then activating your marketing campaign
- If a book, this might mean compiling it into an epub format and uploading it to a digital publisher like kdp
- If a podcast, it might mean outputting the file to mp3 and loading it to your podcast platform
- If a speech, it may mean delivering a speech

I think you get the picture.

After all, this is not rocket science but common sense.

It's important to make sure that your delivery is thoroughly prepared. For example, if you are giving a speech and using PowerPoint slides, make sure your slides and the technology to use these are set up ahead of your speech.

CONCLUSION

To deliver a great piece of communication, you need to:

- Gather your intel
- Structure your message
- Flesh out your structure
- Review your communication piece
- Deliver it

If you work your way through this process, I can guarantee you'll end up with a great piece of communication. You'll have spent the right amount of time defining your message and making sure it is correct before sending it out through the right medium.

This process is deliberately high level because you need to apply it across different types of media. Each media is different and calls on a set of different considerations for maximizing the impact of your message.

In the next section we'll take a quick look at how this process works when using it to write a blog, communicate through a video, and make a post to Facebook.

3
THE METHOD IN ACTION

In this section I'd like to show you how to apply this process to a number of different communication pieces:

- Writing a blog
- Creating a video message
- Posting a Facebook message

To do this, I'll take you through the typical thought process I use when developing a communication piece. I'll capture these thoughts in the following order:

- Purpose
- Audience
- Content
- Medium
- Structure
- Fleshing out

You'll need to have read the previous sections in this book to get the most out of this section. The following graphic provides an overview of what we have covered so far.

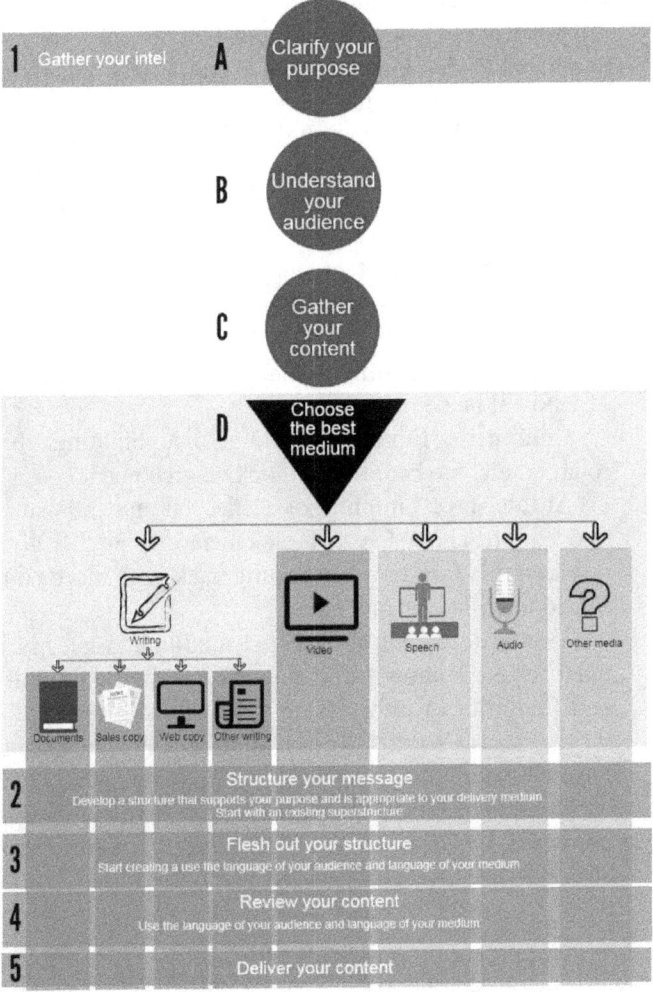

Step 1, gathering your intel, is all about collecting data that will help you choose what media you might like to use.

Steps 2 and onward are about developing your message - guided by your intel - for a specific media output. You'll see this process as we go through each example in this section.

BLOG

Purpose: Explain the benefits of ClickMagick to newbie Internet marketers.

Audience: Newbie Internet marketers. They need to understand why ClickMagick is important and how it can help them. Their attitude – because they are new – is probably of being overwhelmed by all the new stuff they need to learn in the Internet marketing space. They might want to have step by step guidelines. Considering their experience, I'm going to assume that they are computer literate and competent in understanding the Internet. However, they possibly don't know about advanced list building.

Note that the information above helps me to form a picture of who I'll be communicating to.

Content: Email marketing, list building, links and rotators, etc, the benefits of ClickMagick and so on.

At this stage I might look at the list and see that I need to know more about ClickMagick benefits. So I'll go away to research this further maybe come back with more content that I need to collect as raw data.

Medium: A blog is the best medium to get my message out because I know Internet marketers are constantly online and find a lot of information to use from blogs. Since I'll be writing words for the Web, I'll adopt a typical blog style that is conversational and written in plain language.

Structure: Since my purpose is to explain as opposed to convince or instruct, I might use a simple explanation structure like:

- Intro

- The importance of list building in Internet marketing

- The role of clicks and how difficult it is to manage them

- How Click Magic solves a lot of problems

- Describe each problem and how ClickMagick solves them

- Conclusion: ClickMagick is a great tool for list building etc...

Fleshing out: At this point I will flesh out the structure, being careful to use the language of the audience and language of the medium. This means adopting a conversational style, plain language (simple words, short sentences etc), and words that I would expect a newbie Internet marketer to understand.

This requires hard work to flesh out the structure. I am expecting plenty of revisions as I write and re-write the sentences and paragraphs. This is a natural part of the process when fleshing out material. For an article of this size, I'll never be satisfied with what I write the first time around.

During my time fleshing out the structure, I'll need to constantly refer back to my structure and purpose to make sure that what I write stays on course. It may even be necessary to revise some aspects of the structure as I flesh out the material further.

This is the natural order of creating written material.

Review: Since this is a blog that I'm posting myself, I'll probably leave the final draft for a while to think about other things before reviewing it myself. That way I can review with a fresh mind.

VIDEO

Purpose: CEO will explain to company employees (in a bank) a new change to the company structure.

Audience: Company employees in the company (a bank). They need to know about the changes taking place because some roles and responsibilities will change as a result. Staff want to have security in their job.

Content: Old structure, new structure, key changes, why the need for change. Impacts of change etc.

Medium: Video message to be available on the company intranet.

Structure: Company achievements to date, what has worked, what isn't working, what the market is saying, how that affects what we are doing, what we need to change, how we are going to change, what this looks like, encouragement around the great work employees are doing.

Fleshing out: At this stage I will flesh out the structure of a video script for the CEO to read on a video prompt. I'll aim to use language that is plain and uncomplicated, but with words that I know the CEO uses and some phrases that are common to her vocabulary.

Since this is a video, I'll think about images or other video footage that I can use whilst the CEO is talking that emphasizes the points she is making. This allows me to use pictures to tell the story over the text.

I'll also want to keep the script short - ideally within 2 1/2 minutes, because I know that this will work with the general concentration span of a video.

FACEBOOK

Purpose: Let people following me on Facebook know that I've arrived at the latest Mastermind and it is shaping up to be really good.

Audience: People who are following me on Facebook. In this case, it is typically colleagues and students of mine in the field I am working. They are aware that I was travelling and some would have liked to have gone also. No need to explain why I am here etc. They need to stay "connected" with what is happening.

Medium: FaceBook is probably the best medium for this because I can post the information quickly, include a photo and know that the content will be available to those interested fairly quickly. This is social media and so I need to write in a "social" style – no real formality here. That means conversational and "exciting".

Content: What content might be appropriate for me to tell people that I've arrived? Do I have any photos of me or the venue location on arrival? What about details of the arrival, who I might have met etc? I'll pull together whatever I have.

Structure: I think I'll go for a simple structure as per the following:

- Heading – "Just arrived in the Bahamas for the Marketing Mastermind"

- Photo – picture of me on location in Bahamas talking with a famous person who is billed to speak at the mastermind, showing the Caribbean background – this communicates a connection with the speaker, plus a connection with the exotic lifestyle, environment etc.

- Paragraph – Provide a little more detail of who is speaking, why it's exciting, and something about the fun on location outside of the conference

Fleshing out: Time to start writing. So I'll quickly type a heading and some short text before uploading a photo I've decided to use that I know will emphasize the point I'm making. I'll then check it over to make sure the message fits my purpose and reads in the right style. I might tweak this a few times before I'm happy. I'll finally review it and then - when really satisfied - post it.

Special Note:

Earlier in this book, I mentioned that it was important to write down your purpose, audience avatar and pretty much everything in detail. Planning is king before a communication.

But is this necessary when it comes to a simple, quick Facebook post?

The important thing is to have your key intel before starting to write your post. What's your purpose, who is your audience, and what content can you draw from. (No need to consider your medium because you know this already since you're planning to do a post on Facebook.) This key intel might be in your head or you may need to spend some time gathering it. Having this intel means that you can remain focused on your messaging so that it achieves what you want it to.

If this means writing it down, then write it down. Over time, these things should become natural to you. So it won't be that important to write it down as long as you are clear on your purpose and what you want to achieve, who you're talking to and are able to use the language of your audience and chosen medium.

For larger communication pieces it is essential to write the elements down.

CONCLUSION

We've looked at how to apply the process to three media: blogs, video, and Facebook.

There are many more media you can choose from such as giving a speech, presenting a webinar, doing a skype call, or sending a sales email.

You can apply this process to any of these media regardless of what medium you choose. The important thing is to know and use the language of your medium when you get to the point of fleshing out your material.

In the next session I'll take you on a whirlwind introduction to understanding the language of four different media: writing, audio, video, social media and speech making.

4
THE MEDIUM AND ITS LANGUAGE

Earlier in this book I wrote about using the "language of the medium" to communicate your message. This is because each medium has its own language from which it communicates best.

Understanding this language and how to use it will help you communicate effectively in that medium. You'll be able to put extra charge behind your message simply by using the right language for the medium.

What follows is a very high level introduction to a number of media and the language that works well for these.

WRITING

Writing is probably the best medium available to communicate with outside of talking. We use writing for newspapers, documents, brochures, catalogs, emails, social media, the Web and a lot more.

The language of writing comes down to how you choose words, construct sentences and build paragraphs. This leads to different styles such as "plain language", "legaleze", "conversational", "academic" or "salesy".

You can define a style by the elements mentioned above. When reading an academic paper you are likely to see complex words, jargon in long sentences with loads of commas, all within larger than normal paragraphs.

At least when compared with something written in a conversational style. A conversational style will feature simple words, colloquial terms, abbreviations such as "we'll", and short sentences and paragraphs.

Consider writing something technical versus something "salesy". A technical piece of writing will not have adjectives and superlatives that you'll find in a sales letter.

For example contrast "this product removes cobwebs from corners" versus "this amazing product sucks cobwebs from the smallest corners". You can see one is more "salesy" than technical.

As you can see language of writing is all about how you work with words, sentences and paragraphs. Understanding this allows you to identify how good and bad writing works. Then you can emulate the good.

AUDIO

Audio as a communication medium can be typically seen through things like podcasts or radio broadcasts.

The language of audio comes down to what is compelling for the ear. The first kind of mass audio communication was radio, which was described as "theater of the mind".

The audience only has the ear to work with when consuming your message. This makes sound the critical element in creating pictures in the mind.

Those sounds are typically:

- Voice

- Music

- Sound effects

From the voice comes words that interest or bore the listener. Excellent writers for audio use what we call onomatopoeic words. These are words that echo the word's meaning in their sound.

For example, someone "hissing" sounds better than someone "saying". A girl with "fiery red hair" sounds much better than a girl with "red hair". The right choice of words will expand the picture and make it a lot more compelling, thus keeping the listener tuned in to your message.

A word in in itself is not the only way to echo its meaning. The voice and use of expression is an important way to highlight what is important through emphasis, pauses and emotion. This is very powerful in audio.

Music is a great way to create emotions behind a message on audio. Hearing some ska music open the start of a podcast or sit behind a voice over creates a young, positive mood. Change that opening or background music to something out of the "Temple of Doom" soundtrack and you'll have a very different effect.

When choosing music, make sure it reflects both your presentation style and the message you wish to convey.

Finally, sound effects are powerful sounds that can help get the message across. Just think of the rainfall sounds or beach sounds placed behind a voice in the classic relaxation audios. Or roller coaster screaming sounds behind your commentary about the greatest theme parks in the world. We know that attention spans are limited these days. Using a sound effect of a classic "whoosh" between key points in an audio program helps punctuate message and keep people listening.

Why not start listening to some radio programming? Current affairs programs on radio are a good start because they rely on these techniques to keep people listening. Radio drama is also another good source to get ideas of how to communicate effectively through audio. As you hear word choice, voice, music and sound effects in programs, you'll start appreciating how you can use these as well to improve your communication when using audio.

VIDEO

Video is a great medium to deliver a message in today's world. It is easy to consume and easily available everywhere - from computers through to mobile devices and digital display screens that you might find in public places.

The language of video comes down to how you use pictures to tell a story, backed up by audio and some text.

As a communicator you need to start considering how pictures can communicate an idea. A picture in video needs to reinforce whatever is being spoken or texted across the screen.

There is a huge amount of work that goes into communicating through video. You'll need to think about visuals, camera angles when choosing pictures. When editing your work, you'll need to consider punctuation devices like dissolves, fades and crossovers.

Another thing to note about video is that you need to keep images moving to keep people watching. A static screen that doesn't change is boring in the world of viewing video and likely to bore people away from viewing your work.

An excellent book on how to communicate through video is "Rapid Video Development for Trainers: How to Create Learning Videos Fast and Affordably" by Jonathan Halls.

Jonathan Halls is one of the pioneers and leaders in the communication field that promotes an understanding of the medium language as a key to successful communication. Rapid Video Development is essentially a detailed coverage of the language of video that you should read if interested in this area.

SOCIAL MEDIA

Social media is probably one of the most popular communication media today. Whether it is Facebook, Twitter, Instagram or other social platforms, millions around the world share their lives through these platforms.

The language of social media comes down to a mix of text, image and style. For a quick overview of how this works, let's look at Facebook, Twitter and Instagram.

Facebook

Most people use Facebook to share the story of their lives with others. They do this by posting comments, pictures and videos. Facebook is mostly a "happy" medium where content is typically fun and easy going. And very digestible.

A good place to start understanding the language of Facebook is to consider what you wouldn't do when posting:

- Publish a post with ten paragraphs in it

- Post inappropriate images

- Use a detailed and formal language

Doing either of these will actually stop someone from reading your Facebook feed. You'll lose your audience quickly.

A conversational style in your posts, interesting pictures and fun videos work best in Facebook. Staying consistent in your style also helps.

Twitter

Twitter is a quick text medium typically used to update others on what is happening. It's very popular amongst the stars that enjoy a large following but can also be great for smaller community audiences.

The language of Twitter comes down to its writing style. This is short, economical sentences with simple words. The nature of sharing information is to be short and condensed. The subject is usually what one is up to.

To understand why the language works in this way for Twitter, consider what you wouldn't do in Twitter: post a detailed essay.

It's important to remember that Twitter is designed for quick consumption, so you need to package your content for very quick consumption.

Instagram

The language of Instagram is pictures with or without text on them.

You need to be a visual person to work well with Instagram. Find a picture that tells the right story, idea or feeling and post it with a few short words.

PUBLIC SPEAKING

Giving a speech in front of an audience is probably the most popular image people get when they think about being a communicator.

The language of speeches comes down to:

- Content (what you say)
- Verbals (how you use your voice to deliver it)
- Visuals (How you look when you deliver it)

Many experts will suggest that your visuals when giving a speech are the most important element as this is what people will remember after you give the speech. The tone of your voice is next important, followed by the content.

How does this fit with the communication process covered in this book? After all, a considerable amount of time is spent on gathering intel and then structuring the content. If content is the least important element, why spend so much time developing it for a speech?

Good question.

Your content will influence how you deliver your speech both verbally and visually. Without content, your speech will not be coherent.

So it's important to spend time developing your content so that the messaging is right. But you also have to spend a good amount of time getting the voice delivery and your visuals right.

CONCLUSION

Each medium has a different way of delivering a message.

The best way to understand the unique way of delivering a message through a medium is to spend time understanding its language.

This will take learning and applying the skills in this book.

I recommend you choose one medium that you enjoy working with and become an expert in using its language to communicate through it. Read books, watch videos and get coaching in your chosen medium.

Then move on to another medium and do the same with that.

The two elements to being a great communicator are being able to create a clear and concise message and then deliver that well through whatever medium you think will do this best.

Therefore, developing an understanding of as many different media as possible is a critical part of becoming a great communicator.

5
BECOMING A GREAT COMMUNICATOR

This book is an introduction to a way of thinking about communication. It offers you a:

- Framework for understanding how communication works

- Method to follow for creating great communication pieces

- Small taste of the languages different media use in getting a message across

So how is this going to help you become successful in work, play and personal life?

IS COMMUNICATION THE INVISIBLE GLUE?

Communication is a like an invisible glue that connects so many things across all aspects of life, whether it be business, family or social.

A lot has been written around how poor communication has led to some kind of failure.

The Harvard Business Review (October 25, 2012) described a "lax approach to communication management" as a silent killer of business. The poor approach to communication was seen as a reason for big companies failing. [https://hbr.org/2012/10/the-silent-killer-of-big-companies]

The Project Management Institute released the Pulse of the Profession In-Depth Report: "The Essential Role of Communications" back in 2013. The writers argued that poor or substandard communications accounted for more than half of the money at risk on any given project. [http://www.pmi.org/About-Us/Press-Releases/PMI-More-Than-Half-of-All-Project-Budget-Risk-is-Due-to-Ineffective-Communications.aspx]

Let's step out of the business world for a moment and into the personal lives of people. The Huffington Post reported in 2013 that "Poor communication is the #1 reason couples split up" in a report they did on a YourTango survey. [http://www.huffingtonpost.com/2013/11/20/divorce-causes-_n_4304466.html]

Keep looking and you'll find all sorts of problems – personal or business - that were caused by poor communication. Problems that could be prevented by good communication.

Your skill as a great communicator can lead to all sorts of positive outcomes in your personal, business and social life. All you've got to do is put in the work to become a great communicator and practice this across the things in life that are important to you.

STEPS TO BECOMING A GREAT COMMUNICATOR

This book has focused on one element of becoming a great communicator. How to develop the RIGHT message and deliver it to the RIGHT audience.

From reading this book you will have a framework to understand how the important elements of communication work. You'll also have a solid method that takes the framework elements and guarantees a great message and a great delivery.

Communication is not something you become good at overnight. Rather, it is a skill that you continue to develop for the rest of your life.

Here are some suggestions for developing that skill based on the principles in this book:

- Start thinking like a communicator. Remember to consider your purpose and audience whenever you communicate - formally or informally. Watch for signals that tell you more about your audience and adjust your way of delivering the message to suit, always remembering your purpose.

- Initially, this way of approaching things will be slow and cumbersome. But over time with repetition you'll become faster and more natural at applying the winning principles of communication.

- Choose one medium you like and concentrate on becoming great at communicating through that. Written, video, audio, live presentation etc. Then move onto another medium and become great at that one.

- Aim to become competent in communicating through at least three different media.

- Don't stop learning. A great communicator is always looking for better ways of communicating information. You should do the same.

Finally, let me finish by encouraging you to apply the process you've read about in this book:

Get into the habit of gathering your intel before starting any kind of communication. Be clear on your purpose, know who you are targeting, know enough of the available media to choose the best one for your purpose, and gather the right content from which to prepare something meaningful.

Get into the habit of structuring your significant communications.

Enjoy the journey of fleshing out your structure so that you can craft great communications.

Review your work and enjoy the success of delivering it!

UNIVERSITY VALIDATION

The Bullseye methodology has been university validated.

In 2016 Dave Halls and his communication methodology, under the supervision of Dr. Todd Eller, was shown through a university validated study that 302 professors and business owners surveyed stated that Dave Halls' methodology increased productivity 28% to 74%. This methodology is university studied and approved. The significance of the study was conducted using a t-test and was beyond the .05 level. Further studies are being conducted within the developmentally disabled community

In a survey amongst a different group of 52 incoming professors in 2016, *Bullseye! - Getting the RIGHT message to the RIGHT audience*, was rated the number 1 book on communication at the Los Angeles College District between 2010 and 2016. Based on survey research, Bullseye received a 96% score after being used in 2016. This compares to an average score of 68% over the previous five years when other communication text books were used.

For the survey, participants had to use the book and its methodology to prepare and present a communication piece. They then rated the book in terms of its content practicality. They focused on:

1. Clarity
2. Ability to use this method with any audience
3. Usefulness in a real life setting
4. Chance that it will increase their success
5. Helpfulness in teaching their students

This book is now used officially as a communication text book for incoming professors at the Los Angeles College District (the largest college district in the US).

ABOUT THE AUTHOR

Dave Halls is a professional communication expert, author, speaker, entrepreneur, and musician. He has coached and trained countless corporate professionals, entrepreneurs and business owners in communication for over 20 years.

Dave is passionate about sharing his communication expertise, especially to help businesses, entrepreneurs and tech start-ups to succeed.

Dave is a director of his own global company, Halls Global Limited.

Dave is also a successful jazz pianist, composer and band leader. He has released his own original music albums and performed for thousands of people. He is married with two children and lives in Sydney, Australia.

For more information about Dave Halls, please visit davehalls.com.

BONUS RESOURCES

For more information and resources on the Bullseye! communication method, go to:

davehalls.com

DAVE HALLS

www.ingramcontent.com/pod-product-compliance
Lightning Source LLC
Chambersburg PA
CBHW070918180526
45168CB00005B/2051

* 9 7 8 1 5 1 7 2 6 8 0 6 0 *